A QUARTO BOOK

First published in 1984 by Facts On File, Inc.
460 Park Avenue South, New York, N.Y. 10016

Library of Congress Cataloging in Publication Data
Szenasy, Susan S.
Private and executive offices.
(The Office book design series)
Bibliography: p. 94
Includes index.
1. Office layout. 2. Office decoraton.
I. Title. II.Series.
HF5547.2.S93   1983   747′.8523   83-5653

ISBN 0-87196-767-7
ISBN 0-87196-768-5 (pbk.)

PRIVATE AND EXECUTIVE OFFICES
was produced and prepared by
Quarto Marketing Ltd.
212 Fifth Avenue, New York, NY 10010

Editor: Marta Hallett
Art Director: Richard Boddy

Typeset by BPE Graphics, Inc.
Color separations by Hong Kong Scanner Craft Company Ltd.
Printed and bound in Hong Kong by Leefung-Asco Printers Ltd.

Szüleimnek

MY SPECIAL THANKS GO TO
Olga Gueft who showed me that design is a vital
form of communication which is always changing,
sometimes exalting; but at its best, it always
enhances human life, gives dignity to its users,
and respects its environment.

For the opportunity to show how design can
respond to today's needs for privacy at work, I
thank Edith Siroto for recommending me to do
this book.

My sincere appreciation goes to Marta Hallett for
her patient prodding and calm encouragement
through a whirlwind of production deadlines; to
Chris Pullo for her conscientious gathering of
photographs; to Naomi Black for her gentle copy
editing; and to Richard Boddy for his sensitive art
direction.

Thanks also go to Christopher Wilk whose
extensive historical research for a project he and I
co-authored has helped me begin to understand
the development of the office as the modern
workplace.

CONTENTS

Introduction
Where People Matter

PART 1
Executives' Suites
▪ Forest Products Manufacturer ▪
▪ Newspaper Publisher ▪
▪ Investment Consultant ▪
▪ Light Metal and Chemical Engineers ▪
▪ Shopping Center Developers ▪
▪ Investment Builders ▪ Housing Authority ▪
▪ Merchant Bankers ▪ Trading Bankers ▪
▪ Corporate Home and Travel ▪

PART 2
Executives' Offices
▪ Space Planner ▪ Crude Oil Transporter ▪
▪ Assets Manager ▪ Film Producer ▪
▪ Textile Merchandiser ▪
▪ Real Estate Agent ▪ Financier ▪
▪ Branch Bank Managers ▪
▪ Holding Company Executive ▪ Engineers ▪

CONTENTS

Where People Matter

Albert Einstein is the quintessential specialist whose undaunted, lifelong questioning of the physical universe has helped us understand the intricate and complex relationships of all matter, which, subsequently, helped set "spaceship earth" on a more tolerant and caring course.

Design "as if people matter" has a long way to go before the dream is realized. Employers and their designers seem to be content with finding solutions that accommodate job descriptions with cool efficiency. This attitude of designing for abstractions touches all levels of the workplace, confining each position safely to its hierarchical rung. But it's in the general office, designed with no one in particular in mind, that the problem is most plainly seen. While design cannot be blamed for the general malaise of modern society, it adds its own layer of alienation whenever it neglects the individual.

The rapid turnover of workers may puzzle some personnel managers as they walk through attractive offices. But to any worker the message is quite simple: You can be replaced. So the workers wander from work station to work station, in large and medium offices through the land, sometimes decorating their areas with arts and crafts and family photographs. The elusive hope of finding a hospitable place where one can grow and feel important is further confounded by the widespread corporate public relations efforts that promise to recapture the lost home and family in the workplace. But it is only when people discover that they are the major resource of a corporation, that they are meaningful members of teams producing something of value, that their wandering can finally stop. And this sometimes happens in places which pay very little attention to current design trends.

That design can provide well-fitting, personally meaningful workplaces may be seen in private and executive offices where either the funds or the imagination or sometimes both are in abundance. Whether these offices are designed for the solitary worker or a group sharing a project, their message is clear: Persons who work here are important. While job descriptions may dictate some of the general needs routinely accommodated by desks, chairs, storage, lighting, and equipment, each office is also a distinctive expression of the personal style of its occupant or occupants. And because style is so important in conveying to others who we are, the office can become a secondary layer of clothing: Its fine tailoring shows and gets noticed.

But more than appearances, in an educated society, the intellectual challenges and their victorious solutions are generally valued. And such work of the mind requires a great deal of concentration, contemplation, planning, and space to spread out. One of the most important requirements of such work is privacy. The door that can be closed is the simplest and most straightforward solution. Beyond this, there are buffer zones of spaces, things, and people between the worker and unwanted interruptions coming from sounds and movements; access to expansive vistas that can briefly take the mind away from the work and return it refreshed from its solitary wanderings among mountain peaks or city canyons; low light levels that encourage hushed tones while creating a homey, relaxed feeling.

There are also less tangible and much more complex aspects of privacy, one of which psychologists describe as people's perceptions of how much "control" they have over their space and time. Perhaps the best workplaces are those that can create a feeling that is both inclusive and exclusive of other people, part of and apart from a larger area. Maybe what we're after is the fondly remembered attic room where as youthful dreamers we could soar into the future, encouraged and warmed by the familiar sounds of downstairs.

While general offices have had to constantly respond to the technological accommodations of counting, recording, storing, retrieving, and processing information, now known as "data," the private offices have remained relatively untouched by such concerns. As places for decision-making and planning, where talk is more important than "finger dexterity," these offices have for generations followed the household format of library/ study, and in their more expansive forms added dining rooms, parlors, bars, sunporches, baths, kitchens.

But like the home in society, the private office has been constantly threatened by the larger forces in corporations. In 1917, the management expert W. H. Leffingwell began to talk about substituting conference rooms for enclosed offices, in an effort to bring executives and managers closer to the work at hand. These suggestions were as much motivated by a desire to democratize the society of the office as by the high costs of building interior walls and the problems of light and air circulation in pre-airconditioner construction.

But the private office has survived through it all. Its stubborn persistence is perhaps more a signal of entrenched hierarchies that have always needed physical affirmation of subtle status differences, than the recognition that the office with well-defined boundaries is a considerate workplace.

Nothing, it seems, even private offices, could escape the wave of standardizations that began in the 1920s. Then in the 1950s, when corporations consolidated their operations, standards were developed for each position on the organizational chart. While the chairman's Oriental rug and antique desk were sometimes tolerated, the vice-presidents and middle managers were issued "regulation" furnishings that signaled each step to the top. The system of standards persists in a world that somehow doesn't seem quite so receptive to such controlling devices.

The 1950s conformity that was needed to populate the large corporations with "organization men" was considered stifling by the "gamesmen" who broke out of the mold and founded the high-tech companies of the 1970s. Neither the conformist nor the maverick, however, seem to have questioned the morality or added up the social costs of their far-reaching enterprises.

Today's mavericks question just about everything. In fact, they proclaim to be "in revolt against" the rigid institutions and styles of modernism, whether in management or architecture.

These changing times have brought about a new valuation of human resources, even as the material resources that built the industrial society dwindle. Signalling a new phase in the "human potential movement," NASA's space shuttle missions beam to earth the message that there's no room for sexism, racism, and agism in the environment of the future: as a woman, a black man, and an older man float about their jobs in zero-G interiors.

New book titles also indicate a thoughtful exploring of new potentials. *Corporate Cultures* and *In Search of Excellence* study the importance of the nurturing qualities of common goals, real heroes, personal recognition, and social commitment. It seems as if the crucible that fired the 1960s has sent its sparks to ignite the imaginations that are building the "information society." This "data based" world—with its personal computer hook-ups to diverse sources of detailed information—requires people of intelligence, imagination, and a strong sense of ethics.

The corporations that cultivate such workers are exploring ways to challenge highly motivated people. One way is the formation of small, entrepreneurial groups that have total control of their projects. These intense teams are said to give a person a sense of belonging while he/she can shine as a unique contributor. E. F. Schumacher's *Small Is Beautiful* is evoked by such developments. And his words, which began this essay, can conclude hopefully that maybe we are about to redefine work as something "decreed by Providence for the good of man's body and soul." The designs that follow have attempted to consider both.

Executives' Suites

Executives are "like rock stars. People want their minds and their bodies. Because of this, they need to set up some kind of cueing system that determines who can get in to see them and who cannot," says environmental psychologist Ronald Goodrich, who specializes in studying the office because "that's where the action is."

"People at the bottom of the hierarchy are task oriented," explains Goodrich, while at the highest levels they are "role players" who need a stage setting for their work as "idea generators, deal makers, socializers." The middle managers combine task functions with role playing. Corporate environments reflect these divisions by types of jobs in the location, the relative privacy, the quality of furnishings, and the amount of hardware installed in each work space. The higher the position, the less the equipment, the more furniture, space, and privacy.

Partly because executives are seen in a celebritylike role on a world stage where fame is considered the ultimate reward; partly because it's hard to understand why any kind of work should command a seven-figure salary; partly because there's an ongoing attraction/repulsion to the "corridors of power," the executive suite is a constant source of fascination, especially for the nonexecutive.

The executive office, intriguingly enough, can validate personhood. Often set on top floors of buildings, which otherwise seem to be designed for mobs of transients, the executive's suite shows the subtle nuances of personality in its location, its buffer zones of interceptors, its various materials and textures, its size, and its accommodations for social interaction.

While it can be stylish or merely expensive, the executive suite always celebrates success—the solid and lasting kind. This sense of history, this abiding determination to "stay the course," used to be conveyed with antiques, Oriental rugs, damasks, and wood paneling. But as corporations accepted the glass box as their natural environment, as advocates for a "sense of place" called for integrating the exterior with interior styles, and as the marketplace reached a new plateau as a supplier of enormous varieties of custom-made and off-the-floor products, the executive suite became a more interesting design assignment. It could combine the challenges of space planning for a workplace with the more intuitive job of expressing the personality of a wealthy household.

As in a house with many rooms, where the most prestigious chambers are located near the windows, the executive suite has become a laboratory for testing ideas about creating a continuous flow of light throughout a large space with many interior walls. More economical methods than the widely used luminous ceilings with their even, institutional light of the 1950s and 1960s were sought in the energy-conscious years of the 1970s. With a new appreciation for the "natural," designers began in earnest to use the special qualities of daylight as part of a total scheme of color and texture. The translucent wall—whether shoji screen, glass block, etched glass, fiberglass, or clear glass—along with the clerestory, combined with desk lamps, low-intensity incandescent fixtures, and cove lights have contributed to the creation of interiors with considerable warmth, privacy, individuality, and charm.

Contrary to some attempts to attach premature labels to today's design styles (which in any case are better left to historical hindsight), there's a marvelous variety of expressions in current work. The executive suites that follow show a new sensitivity to history, material, texture, color, and light: All express a desire to "humanize the environment." But perhaps the most noticeable difference between these suites and their 1950s and 1960s counterparts is the new joy of craftsmanship, the loving presence of creative hands that formed the furnishings and the artwork.

The executive floor at International Paper is like an enormous house with all the amenities for socializing, solitary work, and support staff. The plan reveals a generous allocation of spaces for **1** elevator lobby, **2** reception area for the executive offices, **3** reception area for the conference/dining room complex, **4** waiting rooms, **5** executive corridor, **6** private phones, **7** boardroom, **8** projection room, **9** kitchen, **10** executive lounge, **11** chairman's dining room, **12** yellow room, **13** executive suite, **14** committee room, **15** future executive office, **16** secretarial offices, **17** executive offices, **18** private washroom, **19** meeting rooms, **20** women's room, **21** men's room. (See pages 10 to 13.)

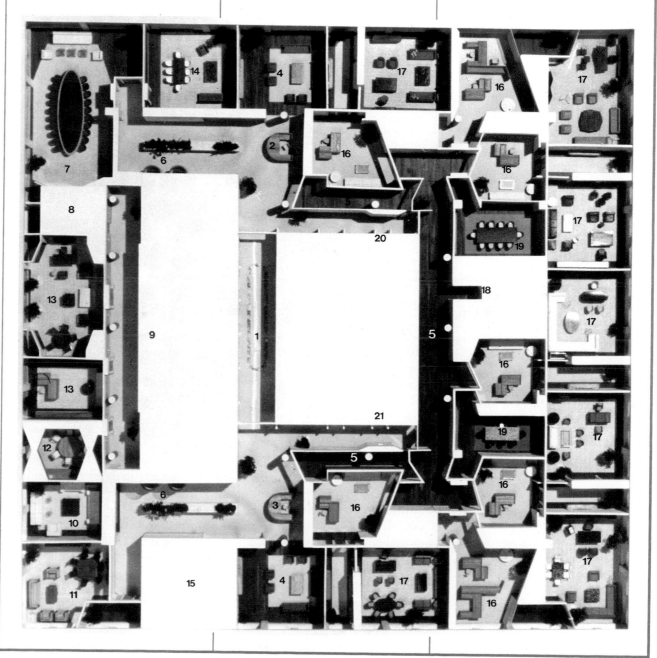

Floor plan courtesy International Paper Company

Forest Products Manufacturer

DESIGN: Space Design Group

Design plays an important role in giving new definition to the "corporate culture" at International Paper. When this giant manufacturer of forest products decided to consolidate its offices in a new headquarters, Dr. Edwin Gee, chairman, saw an opportunity to broadcast a simple message of quality and caring, both inside and outside the company.

Physical reminders of the firm's strengthened convictions are everywhere. The message begins to assert itself on the street (between 44th and 45th streets just east of Manhattan's Avenue of the Americas). Here stands International Paper Plaza, a landscaped surprise amid a busy city block that for years had been going to seed. With its splashing fountain, Tony Smith sculpture, lush foliage, ample outdoor seating, gourmet food service, daily entertainment, and its access to a branch gallery of the American Crafts Museum which rents space on the street level, the Plaza offers both employees and the public a newly enriched

community life, which is the hallmark of any great city. Live music at five p.m. delights passersby as they become temporarily transfixed before descending into the subway.

The International Paper offices begin in an impressive lobby, which people enter from street level by escalators. A security checkpoint directs visitors to the offices, which are equipped with every amenity a modern corporation can now proudly offer its employees: spacious and well-lit work areas, meeting and staff training rooms, a well-equipped fitness center, a theater, product exhibits, a reference library, and reminders of the artistic nature of wood and paper in the works of excellent contemporary artists on display throughout the offices.

But it is on the executive floor, with its magnificent midtown Manhattan views and generous division of 34,500 square feet among seven executives, that the International Paper message of quality and caring is most apparent. Essentially, the

On either side of the elevators on the 44th floor, a spacious reception area and waiting room welcomes visitors as they are announced to the surrounding executive offices.

Serving as an art gallery, the main executive corridor, with its powerful progression of zebra-wood columns, contains a paper collage by Maud Morgan and wood sculptures by Pino Pedano. The corridor displays major pieces in the International Paper collection gathered by Plum Gee, the chairman's wife.

Photographs: Mark Ross

floor is planned as a symmetrical sculpture with identical reception and waiting areas on either side of the elevators. The executives' offices, roughly equal in size, are lined up around the perimeter of the curtain wall, each in a high-status position. Two of the corners have been neutralized: one is occupied by the enormous boardroom, another by the chairman's dining room. The other two corners house the chairman and the president.

The chairman who is often seen pressing the palm, politician-style, at the office's entrances, in encounter group sessions with employees, or while touring one of the factories around the country, is convinced that his personal involvement in the design of the offices is essential to his job of "culture building." To the business community, the message delivered by the interior spaces and fittings is clear: "We are enormous, expansive, and here to stay."

In addition to the obligatory boardroom, series of committee rooms, and the executive washroom with showers and sauna, International Paper has one of the finest private restaurants in New York. A resident chef, wine steward, and waitress serve business dinners at least twice a week, and luncheons more frequently. With Broadway below, the New Jersey Meadowlands across the Hudson, and the tactile surfaces of George Nakashima's soulful furniture at hand, this is truly a "theater of operations," as the designer Marvin Affrime likes to call all the executive offices that his firm, the Space Design Group, creates for such powerful corporate clients.

The boardroom is equipped with a rearview projection screen that is concealed behind panels at the viewer's end of the vast space.

Detail of the walnut dining table highlights its butterfly inlays and velvety surfaces.

Like a living room, the executive lounge is designed for comfortable conversation, but its spaciousness clearly extends its use for businesslike exchanges. The red lacquer of the table is repeated inside the bar.

Photographs: Mark Ross

Newspaper Publisher
DESIGN: Environmental Planning & Research

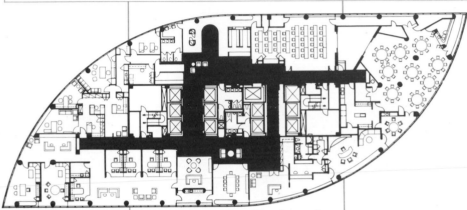

The curving, seed-podlike shape of the building by architects Hellmuth, Obata, Kassabaum provides a natural flow of windowed space for the entire executive suite.

Beyond the reception area to the executive floor is the conference room and the chairman's private waiting area. The glass walls of both can be closed off with the venetian blinds. Artworks on paper, from the holdings of Washington's Renwick Gallery, are changed twice a year.

It's not surprising that Allen Neuharth's favorite color is newsprint. Black and white, that is. As chairman/president of the Gannett papers, he recently launched the newspaper *USA Today*, now sold at busy street-corners from dispensers that resemble television sets.

Neuharth oversees the Gannett communications empire from his executive suite at the headquarters' offices of the new paper in Arlington, Virginia. Here, the word sophisticated refers to much more than the chairman's impeccable personal style. Designed with the elegant materials of granite, leather, and lacquer, the suite is equipped with elegance of another kind: the most advanced electronic devices for communicating as well as for guarding privacy.

This hardware does not merely reflect an interest in gadgetry. Electronics are now used to produce daily papers. And *USA Today*, produced on five floors below the chairman's suite, was planned from the outset as an enterprise that would employ "state of the art" technology in all its phases, including writing and editing.

The same rational efficiency that is a prerequisite to making the machines run is evident in the design of the chairman's office. Positioned between the conference room and the dining room, the suite of offices follow the simple arc of the building's contours and provide the essentials for modern communication: for discussions at short and long distance, reading the printed word and viewing electronic images, and even the capability to shut it all off by a push of the button.

Floor plan courtesy Hellmuth, Obata, Kassabaum

The chairman's private dining room adjoins his office and the gourmet kitchen that also serves the large dining room beyond.

The chairman's private office consists of a simple desk/console arrangement with a slight difference: It includes television screens set into the cornice facing the desk and a hydraulic newspaper reading stand built into the credenza below. A constant reminder of the Gannett papers' enormous reach, an illuminated map behind the desk pinpoints all the periodicals' outposts. Digital clocks overhead mark the time in each zone. Draperies and doors can be opened and shut from the desk. The lighting is also controlled automatically.

Photographs: Peter Aaron © ESTO

Investment Consultant

ARCHITECT:
Arthur Gensler & Associates

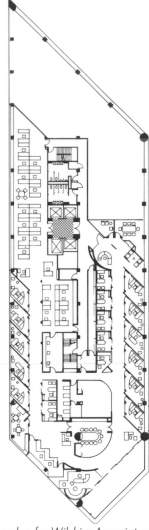

The plan for Wilshire Associates uses a simple, U-shaped circulation pattern. The terrace and president's office are located at the bottom tip.

There are eleven vice-presidents at Wilshire Associates, an investment consulting firm in Santa Monica, California. Equal in status, equally in need of visual and acoustic privacy, each executive is angled into a rhomboid-shaped office that recalls the contours of the long and relatively narrow building. The 45-degree angling of the dividing walls was designed as much for visual privacy as for the need to fit 46 workers into a relatively small space (13,000 sq. ft.) without squeezing them.

The perimeter executive offices are open on one side to coastal or mountain views, on the other to the inner offices with which they share natural light and views. Their glass walls cleverly avoid the dreaded "fishbowl effect" by the placement of console-type desks that block direct eye-contact with the hallways.

An open terrace overlooks the Pacific Ocean. So all the employees may enjoy this special amenity of contemporary office life, only the president's office was built along the glass wall of the terrace. The chief executive is discreetly niched into a triangular space, taking up only a small portion of the communal view.

A spacious office has been created for the president at the tip of the building by using built-in lounge-seating and shelving. The pastel colors here and throughout reflect all the warmth and crispness of the California seacoast.

One of the vice-president's offices as seen from the hall. The glass wall lets sunlight enter the interior offices, while the angle of the dividing walls and console protect his privacy.

Photographs: Jaime Ardiles-Arce

Light Metal and Chemical Engineers

ARCHITECT: Samuel J. de Santo

Ceremonious reception is underscored by the massive, marble desk with undulating curves, the glass and mirror of the latticed wall that reveals the private staircase beyond, and the marble monoliths that send their light upward to the open ceiling plane. The rippled form of Lisa Roggle's white sculpture and the circular shapes of Eileen Gray's chrome tables soften the grid.

Alusuisse, a worldwide business built on modern materials and technologies—metals, chemicals, and engineering—is a perfect host to this century's important design ideas. The office of the company's American headquarters are located on the top two floors (26 and 27) of an I. M. Pei building in New York City and furnished with the work of such outstanding design talent as Le Corbusier (sofas); Mies van der Rohe, Charles Rennie Mackintosh, and Charles Eames (chairs); Eileen Gray and Joseph D'Urso (tables); and Tobia Scarpa (sconces).

A simple, modern grid, inspired by the building's exterior, is used throughout the executive offices, both as a planning device and as a design detail.

The floor plan is a straightforward arrangement of square and rectangular offices and conference rooms along the curtain walls and the interior halls. Each office provides an enclosed space, yet each, even those along the interior corridors, receives natural light and offers grand urban views to its occupants. This amenity was chosen over the visual privacy of opaque walls, which occur only in the office of the vice-president

of American operations.

The storage walls that separate the offices, and in some cases hide structural columns, are paneled in "Alucabond," an anodized aluminum surfacing material made by an Alusuisse subsidiary. This neutral gray surface changes colors throughout the day, from the bluish cast of morning to the oranges and pinks of sunset.

The grid as a decorative detail appears in the lobby's marble floor, the reception area's latticed wall, the pattern of the ceiling and the carpet, the backs of the Mackintosh chairs, and the cushions of the Corbu sofas.

The vice-president's office, set into the building's chamfered corner, has a solid wall, lined with storage facilities that promise complete privacy. The two distinct areas of the office—sitting (with its Corbu sofas and Eileen Gray lamp) and working (with its granite-top D'Urso table)—are defined by the subtle grid pattern woven into the carpet.

Two small interior conference rooms on the 26th floor have glass walls that let in the natural light and command views of the New York skyline as well as of the offices on either side.

At the second-floor landing a slab has been taken out of the waffled floor, thus revealing a construction detail and visually connecting the two levels of the offices.

Shopping Center Developers

ARCHITECTS: Hambrecht Terrell International

All of the offices on the senior executive floor are private. The principals of the firm, housed in the triangular point of the building, are removed from the general traffic of the floor, which is occupied by legal, financial, development, and leasing departments.

Floor plan courtesy Hambrecht Terrell International

The center of power at Melvin Simon Associates is located in the sharp-edged corner of the Indianapolis Merchants' Plaza. The three Simon brothers conduct their shopping center developing business from spacious, multiuse offices here. Occupying a good portion of the senior executive floor, one of four floors at the 80,000-square-foot corporate headquarters, the brothers' offices have grand interior and exterior vistas.

A trip to their protected corner serves as a reminder of the basic ingredients of shopping center development: a success-prone location, an inventive use of space, memorable architecture, and grandness with personal appeal.

From the triangular reception area that services the entire floor, the Simons' private reception area is reached through a corridor distinguished by a continuous band of light that zigzags across the ceiling, following the line of the angled walls. This lighting solution creates an optical illusion that makes the trip down the hall appear shorter than it really is.

In the private reception area, the expansive facet of the Melvin Simon corporate image is reconfirmed. This bright, open space is merely a prelude to the generous offices of the three principals.

Each office is fitted with the materials that best reflect the personality of its occupant, while maintaining a high-quality corporate image: polished woods and marbles, luxurious wools and silks, and valuable art collections that rotate between the offices and museums.

The various types of meetings and entertainment that define the ways of working here are accommodated by level changes in the ceilings and floors which niche or expand spaces within rooms. The traditional symbol of office work, the desk, is surrounded by the realities of executive work: meeting areas with comfortable seating, bars, video-viewing rooms, and a protective layer of personnel stationed at every entry point.

The private reception area to the Simon brothers' offices is anchored by the building's structural column, which is highlighted by a bronze cladding.

The suite of Herb Simon contains two generous sitting areas: one on a raised platform, another in a lowered niche. Here several meetings may go on at once. Each area can be entered by its own door or from within.

Photographs: Michael Datoli

Herb Simon chose light woodworking—English sycamore—to set off his Picassos, Mirós, and Calders. Hans Wegner's peacock chairs add a strong, sculptural presence to the fine craftsmanship of this impressively scaled room.

Fred Simon often meets with large groups that need a large, level space in which to congregate. The separation between work area and conference area is suggested by a change of materials only. The Rojo Alicante marble floor gives way to the wool-carpeted lounge area. The walls are cherry paneled, displaying to advantage Robert Indiana's painting commissioned for the company's twentieth anniversary.

Photographs: Michael Datoli

Melvin Simon wanted a red office. French Rose marble and African Kavazinga paneling provide a warm sense of well-being here. The traditional office work-area, with its desk and video screens, is distinguished from the lounge area by a level change that's reinforced by a material change from hard marble to soft carpet.

Investment Builders

DESIGNERS:
Bromley / Jacobsen Architecture and Design

The major transactions take place over the executives' desks at Cohen Brothers Realty and Development in New York City. Because the desk is used like a "bargaining table" by these investment builders, it was designed to combine the function of a work surface with that of a conference table.

The brothers both work at their six-foot-wide marble tables, the major piece of furniture in their spacious offices with gratifying views of the skyline they helped build. Each of the four junior executives' offices, which are sandwiched between the two senior offices, are equipped the same way, on a less grand scale.

Each office is usually closed to all the others, but at lunch time their occupants meet in the conference/dining room, served from the adjacent kitchen.

Adding to the feeling of respectful privacy is the low-level, incandescent lighting throughout. Only the four secretarial work stations in the open plan have fluorescent task lights. The intimate character of this exective suite is further conveyed by the warm, fleshy colors and the massive, rounded columns (some structural, some merely decorative) that stand as silent reminders of stability.

Edward Cohen chose a square table. The marble floors, the massive columns, the heavily gridded ceiling, and the delicate silk fabric walls give these offices a feeling of lasting quality.

At the reception desk, golden trowels inscribed with the statistics of their important buildings celebrate the Cohen Brothers' nearly three decades of successes.

Photographs: Stan Ries © ESTO

Sherman Cohen preferred the round desk. From a small credenza by his chair, he can lock his door electronically.

Luncheons are regularly served in the conference room from the adjoining kitchen. A pivoting table hidden in the wall shared between the service area and the conference room eases the serving process.

The secretarial stations create a corridor by the bank of enclosed offices. The privacy of these stations is guarded by the column of light that emanates from the tops of the partitions in this softly lit room.

Housing Authority

DESIGNERS: Neville Lewis Associates, Inc.

Because the Malo Mansion is a landmark structure, the exterior renovations were limited to the architectural details.

By its location in a restored mansion on Denver's historic Capitol Hill, the Colorado Housing Authority announces itself as a progressive, open-minded agency. It is operating in a generously pluralistic environment where the impulse to tear down is often challenged by the desire to restore, renovate, and re-use buildings that would have been wiped away only a decade ago. Thus, historical awareness has become a sign of caring for the environment.

The Malo Mansion, built almost a century ago in a Spanish revival style, was a delight for the restorers who have respectfully kept its intricate moldings, trims, and woodwork intact. Very little of the original layout was changed; only the functions of the rooms are different.

The grand entrance is still a reception area, the dining room has become a boardroom, the sunporch works well for small meetings, and the library is a comfortable director's office.

In keeping with the traditional concerns of domestic architecture for privacy that occasionally seeks society, the adapted offices are guarded by doors; the meeting places are sunny and generous. The spirit of the old building has been kind to its new occupants.

The first impression is a lasting one at the general reception area, with its grand entrance, welcoming fireplace, and elegant moldings.

The executive director has access to the boardroom and small conference room from his office.

Photographs: Ron Johnson/Imageworks

Merchant Bankers

ARCHITECT:
Emilio Ambasz

The bank's main hall on the ground floor, although a rather small room (8 m. x 12 m.) with a low ceiling, is made spacious by the minimal use of furniture and three trompe l'oeil windows. The layered appearance of the mountains is achieved by three cut-out panels of differing heights (30 cms. apart) illuminated from within by hidden lights that can vary in intensity.

Here in Lausanne, Switzerland, as in many densely built cities, the countryside that was once visible from the streets is now but a whispering memory. Buildings crowd one another and block out the surrounding alpine peaks. Quaint façades are seldom seen in their full glory from the narrow streets. But an ingenious design solution can sometimes bring back both the misty mountains and the hidden architecture. At the same time, it can present a foreign business as a considerate neighbor that is sensitive to its surroundings.

This is just what happened at the Belgian Bruxelles Lambert bank's Lausanne branch offices. The ground floor, where customers first enter the bank, evokes a sense of being in a peaceful valley surrounded by craggy mountains and gauzy clouds. This artistic rendering of the once-visible landscape uses paint, light, and silk threads. A reminder of the city street is the

architectural model of the building's façade, here used as a sculpture that actually hides a door. The sense of privacy, serenity, and luxury has been made to appeal to the dignified merchants who bank here.

The executive offices on the fifth floor restate the memorable atmosphere of the main hall in the less theatrical, more businesslike waiting areas, offices, meeting rooms for clients, and two boardrooms. The simple black-and-white color scheme with touches of red reappears here. But the most intriguing design detail is in the lighting solution, introduced with the trompe l'oeil walls of the ground floor. Strips of lights around the ceiling are hidden from view by layers of silk thread that cover the walls and diffuse the light— creating walls of misty light, as it were. There was no need to re-create mountains or buildings on the fifth floor; the windows bring in the real city.

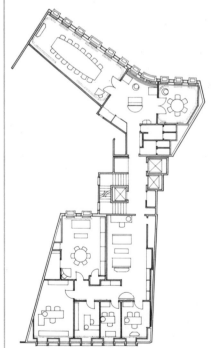

Plan of the fifth floor executive offices.

Floor plan courtesy Emilio Ambasz

The two Carrara marble counters, where the bank's customers write up their transactions, are angled to correspond with the direction of the bronze strips on the floor, whose vanishing-point perspective gives an illusion of depth to the small room. The inlaid strips culminate at the architectural model of the building's façade, which hides the door to a room where the safe deposit boxes are kept. The light reflected in the highly polished surfaces of the minimal furnishings gives each piece a special, abstract quality of its own.

The Lausanne cityscape can be seen through the fifth floor windows. Here, as throughout the bank, there is no need for overhead lighting, as torcheres dapple the ceilings and walls, and the desk lamp illuminates the work.

The light walls made of fixtures around the edges of the ceiling and silk threads are especially dramatic in the sparely furnished boardroom with its reflective, high-lacquer tabletop.

The efficient progression of the executive corridor is softened by the delicate silk-lined walls and occasional table lamps' pool of light.

Trading Bankers
ARCHITECTS: Rivkin Weisman

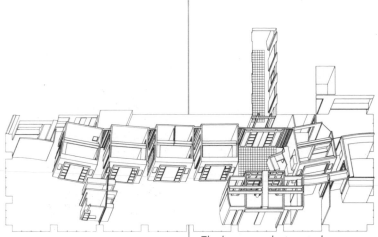

The large, undesignated spaces are open-plan. The chief executive occupies the corner office at the lower right.

At the reception area, the glass wall of the conference room and the mirrored ceiling give the impression of wide-open spaces. A sculptured screen, painted in earthy pinks, blocks direct view into the glass-walled conference room.

At Credit du Nord's New York offices, it was not the senior executives who got the new furniture but the managers and the staff. The director of this Paris-based bank, which trades currencies, precious metals, and commodities, chose a corner location with a view, directly adjacent to the reception and conference room, and furnished it with his own things.

The managers who are responsible for the everyday operations of the bank needed privacy for their paperwork, telephoning, and conferencing, but also had to be very much part of the general communications on the office floor.

The gently angled row of offices with their glass windows that front the open staff area provide a quiet workplace that protects verbal exchanges, yet encourages visual signals between managers and their team of workers.

The opaque glass, latticed into either side of the clear pane, adds to the feeling of privacy but does not subtract from the necessity of eye-contact. Although lit from within, each enclosed office also receives light from the windows. The staff, while enjoying the feeling of daytime light changes, faces away from the windows, toward the managers' offices. The creative daydreaming set in motion by the city's canyons seems to take part only in the director's job description.

When the projection screen is not in use, it is back-lit by showcase lights that add to the room's sculptured quality, as do the pilasters, pediments, and beams. Cove lighting is supplemented by sconces.

A manager's office has a "picture window" decorated with an opaque glass screen on each side. The exterior walls of enclosed offices are burnt-orange tile as are the walls of the reception area.

Photographs: Peter Aaron © ESTO

Corporate Home and Travel

DESIGNERS:
Kenneth Parker Associates (Home)
Sandra Nunnerly (Travel)

The corporate residence extends the executive suite. It provides a home away from home for officers who frequently visit their regional outposts. Such is the case at the ARCO Chemical and Research Center in Newton Square, Pennsylvania, where a new facility for an 800-member staff of mostly engineers sprawls across a 60-acre sylvan site called The Meadows.

When the president of ARCO comes to stay, he lives in a comfortable home that's especially furnished for his needs as head of a giant chemical corporation. The house is arranged as a series of spacious rooms that freely flow into one another, welcoming guests for friendly, though doubtless powerful, gatherings. The message of hospitality is in the warm colors, the generous seating arrangements, the good food, and the charming artifacts that acknowledge the aesthetic importance of Pennsylvania craftsmen.

The same workmanlike, efficient unpretentiousness that marks Amish crafts, which also decorate the main office complex, is found in this home on the corporate enclave. The message of hard work and its rewards is clear and reassuring.

The president's guest house is one of nine fieldstone cottages at The Meadows. They were built a century ago and subsequently became a girl's school whose president preceded ARCO's president in the house. The other cottages on the property, now also renovated, are guest residences for other visiting executives and engineers. The living complex is maintained by a resident couple who run it like a good hotel.

Photographs (home): Tom Crane

Although teleconferencing clearly has its place in the executive suite, when it comes to major decisions about people and policies, personal contact is still the best way to get things done. One essential link that connects fellow powerbrokers is the corporate airplane. While some people see it only as the ultimate status symbol, others note that it's a convenient and private alternative to public transportation. While the furnishings and technical apparatus may be regulation, the materials used can make the difference between a quality flight and an average trip. On this Mitsubishi MU 2L, all the materials are natural: fine leather on the seats and ceiling panels, wool fabrics on the ceilings and windows, and wool carpet on the floors. A high-grade laminate covers the flip-top tables and cabinetry. All materials mcct FAA standards for fire retardancy. These materials also meet standard requirements for personal comfort, sound absorption, maintenance/durability, and weight.

Executives' Offices

Whether surrounded by a suite of offices, conference rooms, corridors, dining rooms, bars, kitchens, gyms, and saunas or simply placed next to a small support staff, the executive office is usually arranged in the tradition of a home study.

But the old home was never quite like this. The privacy necessary for meetings as well as personal work time is given a new dimension by the growing use of electronic technology in the executive's office. Within his or her reach are the controls for changing the texture of the room by closing curtains, dimming lights, providing background music, or summoning the staff.

While not all executive offices are so electronically inclined, all of them need to accommodate the many meetings that seem to take up a large part of the workday. The traditional three-tiered office (soft seating, conference table, and desk area) is currently under attack in the business press for its waste of space, its redundancy, and its ostentatious luxury in face of the lean-and-mean look that's supposed to be appropriate for managers charged with "trimming the fat."

Although three-tiered offices are still being designed, more common are the two-tiered arrangements with only a conference area and a desk area. Depending on the work style of the executive, this might mean a soft seating group near the desk, a set of visitors' chairs that can be turned from the desk to expand the lounge area's seating spaces, or the two work-surface approach of using a desk and a conference table.

A more bare-bones solution uses a large desk with either a square or a round top, surrounded by chairs and sofas. But even in such democratically inclined offices, there's never any doubt about who is in charge: The executive's chair is either bulkier, taller, or more mobile than the others.

Proving that banking is a personal business, the chairman of the Continental Bank does most of his work in the lounge/conference area where he discusses financial arrangements with clients from a variety of industries. The obligatory desk is mostly for show. Actual paperwork is done in the chairman's private office, which is adjacent to this large "living room." The traditional components of executive office design have been used to achieve an atmosphere of substance, quality, and power. Wood paneling, leather club chairs, and antique Oriental rug are a surprising departure in style from the bank's monumental modern appearance which, as a member of the second largest holding company in Texas, is the major tenant (200,000 sq. ft.) in the Continental Plaza in Fort Worth. DESIGN: ISD Incorporated

Crude Oil Transporter

The owner's office takes up one-sixth of the 6,000-square-foot office space of Globtik Tankers (USA), an English transporter of crude oil. This corner office provides a luxurious version of traditional executive office arrangements: The conference table with its Italian "Rosso Inferno" marble top occupies a distinctly formal area that is defined by the bleached Australian oak floor. The large Kirman carpet brings together the soft seating and the working areas, which are furnished in the navy, rust, and cream colors of the carpet. The elm-burl desk's left-hand drawer contains a control panel for telephone, intercom, room temperature, lights, the sliding doors on either side of the room, stereo, and window drapery. The credenza contains two closed-circuit televisions that also receive all conventional channels. The paneled wall conceals a bath on one side, a kitchen on the other.
ARCHITECT: Christopher H.L. Owen

Space Planner

As more buildings with interesting forms are being designed, the interior spaces present new challenges to planners brought up on the modern grid. Showing their ability to adapt, this Dallas space planning firm chose to occupy just such a newfangled building. Here a staff of seven planners and designers each has a corner office, one in each notch of the saw-tooth curtain wall. The president occupies three notches. His office arrangement is simply a long table, assembled from the modular elements of Bruce Burdick's furniture system, centered to the interior glass wall in such a way to signal that the chief is available for brief conferences. The more private segment of this glass-walled office is in the notch that holds the tele-communications equipment, reference files, and small work surfaces. The third notch has a low, blocklike, lounge, seating group for quick and efficient conversations.
DESIGN: Neville Lewis Associates

Assets Manager

Private conferences are frequent during the work day of the president of Merrill Lynch Assets Management in New York City. The traditional three-area office has been simplified by turning the soft-seating unit to face the desk, thus giving conversations a relaxed yet definitely serious character imposed by the distances and the neutral territory of the desk. The formal conference table to one side is centered about a white polyester resin-finished cabinet that contains a bar and additional storage space. The occupant's interest in Oriental art is reflected in the latticed window treatments, the Oriental-style armchairs, the simple mahogany desk and credenza, and the sparingly used but rich-in-design artwork. Incandescent down lights cast a warm shadow over the area. DESIGNERS: The Miller Organization.

Film Producer

The highly personal and "bi-coastal" nature of the movie business requires a relaxed and private atmosphere as well as an environment that can cater to the heavy phone contact between New York and Los Angeles. Kathrin Seitz, vice president of CBS Films, often receives writers, directors, and actors in her New York office. For these meetings, she comes around her desk to the lounge area where idea exchanges take on an informal character that appeals to creative people. The soft lighting heightens the "living room" informality of these meetings. Corner views, soft colors, and a general lack of clutter provide the "mental space" needed for thinking quickly during phone conversations. The desk, which some call her "tower of power," was specially designed to reinforce the importance of her position.
ARCHITECTS: Voorsanger & Mills

Photographs: Peter Aaron © ESTO

Textile Merchandiser

The office of the founder and president of Gretchen Bellinger Inc., a New York-based textile design firm, is centrally located on the floor of a converted loft space. Natural light, which pours in through the generous windows to the open workspace, is brought into this large, enclosed room by a clerestory. The organization for the various work functions is a straightforward, symmetrical layering of a built-in credenza, a desk with two visitors' chairs, and two sofas facing one another in a somewhat less formal conference/lounge area. In addition to the elegant fabrics she produces, such as "Limousine Cloth," which covers the sofas, Bellinger displays her infallible sense of modern design in her choice of furniture: Mies van der Rohe chairs, sofas, and desk specially made of East African rosewood.
SPACE PLANNER: Powell Kleinschmidt.

Real Estate Agent

An interior glass-block wall adds a third light emitting surface to the corner office of the president of Judson Realty in New York City. The elegant simplicity is achieved by keeping the furnishings to a few essential pieces: a glass-top table with facing executive and visitors' chairs, a built-in banquette for additional seating at right angles to the table, and closet space for storage. Warm fluorescent strips and incandescent wall-washers are hung from the ceiling where the pipes have been left exposed and the ducts are painted a mulberry color.
ARCHITECT: Christopher H.L. Owen

Photograph: Norman McGrath

Financier

A New York financier for developers converts his small office into a conference room by turning the visitors' chairs to face the couch. Traditional in form, contemporary in finish, the office successfully brings together two seemingly opposing images: stability and dynamism. The Chippendale reproduction desk and chairs were bleached and rubbed with a pale-gray finish that gives these eighteenth-century forms a contemporary appearance. The antique lamp casts a pool of warm light on the desk surface, while the room is washed in a soft light from the illuminated soffit under the curved ceiling. The swag-and-festoon window treatment, the keystones from old buildings that decorate the wall, the stone-based glass coffee table all place this office in the late twentieth-century, a time of renewed interest in historical styles.

INTERIOR DESIGN:
Charles Swerz & Assoc.

Photograph: Frank B. Ritter

Branch Bank Manager

The Banca Nazionale del Lavoro, Italy's largest bank, has a number of offices in North America. In the Midwest, the bank's vice-president/ manager receives corporate clients in his office's conference/lounge area. The reasonably small interior space is made a more powerful place for doing business by its generous views of the Chicago skyline and the elegant use of lasting materials like marble and leather.

INTERIOR DESIGN:
ISD Incorporated

Photograph: David Clifton

Branch Bank Manager

The grand baroque façades and colonnades of Turin, Italy, are recalled in the dramatic architecture and furnishings in the New York offices of the Sanpaolo Bank. The manager conducts business from an impressive setting composed of an altarlike credenza and an extravagant desk from which he can adjourn to sit at the less picturesque conference table with its marble top.
ARCHITECTS: Voorsanger & Mills

Holding Company Executive

The executive vice-president of a New York holding company can move work from the office desk to a round conference table that seats six comfortably. A custom-made oak credenza that faces the desk keeps reference books within sight and provides storage for papers and coats. Beyond the oak-and-marble conference table, a gray column conceals a shower, which is part of this office's private water closet facilities.
ARCHITECTS: Gwathmey Siegel

Photographs: Jaime Ardiles-Arce

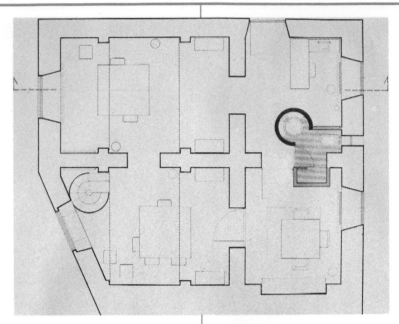

Engineers

The usual layering of status symbols does not appear in the Termotecnica offices in Rome, Italy. Converted from an old building, the offices are a series of similarly furnished rooms where bare white walls and ceilings, shiny red accents, and slate-color floors host minimal furniture in a serene setting.

Acoustically and visually protective walls with arched pass-throughs connect the major rooms. One room, completely private, can be closed off by two doors. The major piece of furniture in each office is a large, square desk which becomes a conference table.

Open spaces are painted white, furnished with white desks. The private areas are painted black.

Part of the mezzanine, seen from an arched passageway, forms the partial ceiling of the two offices beneath. The draftsmen's tables that overlook the offices·below are lodged under the vaulted ceiling of the balcony, which is reached by a spiral staircase.

The plan reveals the round, red column at one end, part of the new washroom, diagonally across from a red spiral staircase that leads to the mezzanine.
ARCHITECTS: Ascarelli, Macciocci, Nicolao, Parisio.

Floor plan courtesy of the architects

Photographs: Janos Grapow

Specialists' Workrooms

In corporations populated by many powerless people the private office in the executive suite is a sign of power. For professionals, small businesses, and people who insist on having a room of their own, the private office is perhaps a less symbolic but more practical workplace. A person whose work cannot progress without close cooperation, confidentiality, and solitude has always opted for the more intimate environment. The physician, the attorney, the writer, and the artist are all naturally drawn to it.

Perhaps because of either a deep-rooted cultural memory or a personal association of the home with comfort, intimacy, and an accepting group of related people, the domestic model of the office seems to be stronger than ever. It is occupied by a wide variety of personalities involved in highly specialized work. There are those who lead seamless lives that allow no boundaries of space and time between work and play, pleasure and business. The most receptive workplace for such people seems to be the house, the apartment, the loft. Here rooms may be set aside for working, but the spirit of creativity is in evidence everywhere.

Some people prefer to draw a definite line of separation between their office and domestic lives, but opt to work at home for reasons that might be as basic as privacy, convenience, or economics. The separation of the two lives lends itself to an interesting architectural problem of accommodating circulation—to prevent the domestic and the business traffic from bumping into one another. Therefore, the separate entrance to a room away from the main circulation of the household, and the various methods of lighting the interior and shading it from its surroundings provide for the privacy needs of adjacent areas.

In addition to adapting former domestic buildings for offices, designers are creating that intimate scale over and over in spaces that are neutral and expansive. Whether it is a group of individual, self-sufficient labs set inside a large, cavernous building or evocations of garden houses—in styles as varied as country French or Japanese—these offices never neglect that "sense of place" that helps a person locate himself or herself in a world of many conflicting signals.

A biologist at the neurology lab at Cold Spring Harbor (see page 69) plants electrodes in the nerve cells of leeches. His sensitive research work needs a completely isolated room where heat, sound, and movement are carefully controlled.

Equal Partners

ARCHITECTS: Gwathmey Siegal

The partners each have an 11-foot-long desk, backed by a built-in storage wall.

For a dozen years after they formed what subsequently became one of the legendary modern partnerships in architecture, Charles Gwathmey and Robert Siegel shared a desk in their much-publicized offices in New York's picturesque Carnegie Hall. Recently, when they moved their expanded practice to a Tenth Avenue loft, which nearly tripled the firm's floorspace, the partners decided that a shared office still suited their way of working. Now they face one another from equal corner desks, overlooking a small, central lounge area.

Their offices showcase the Gwathmey Siegel attitude toward the use of materials. In keeping with an egalitarian philosophy that a person should feel part of the "overall, not part of the hierarchy," the offices throughout are furnished with white laminate-clad work and storage units. Classic modern chairs—the message of quality contained in their simple forms as much as in their universally available materials—are at home throughout this unpretentious environment. There is nothing exclusive about the private office; its "upgrading" is signaled here by both its acoustical privacy and its separation.

The conference room is equipped with audio-visual projectors, as well as plentiful open- and closed storage space for presentations of ideas and material samples.

The reception area displays models of the firm's buildings. The waiting area includes a banquette, which is niched into an alcove that is decorated with a trompe l'oeil mural of a glass-block wall, a favorite material of these well-known architects.

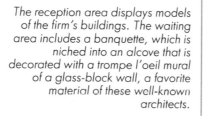

Photographs: Jaime Ardiles-Arce

Artists at Heart

ARCHITECTS:
Salvati Tresoldi

The open spaces washed everywhere by the light of the Lombardy sun, the visual delight of pastel-colored architectural forms that appear like abstract sculptures in space, the expansive floors and ceilings with their warm and reassuring wood grains, the mysteriously floating sculptures, and the minimal use of furniture all work together to create an atmosphere of playfulness in Salvati Tresoldi's highly utilitarian architecture studio in Milan.

The lofty room is cut into two separate levels by a mezzanine. The open drafting area on the first floor has access to the upper-level presentation rooms and private offices through a spiral staircase that winds around a cylindrical column. This same cylinder shape is used throughout to support long, narrow tables where large architectural drawings can be spread out.

The only thing that distinguishes the private office from the rest of the space is its low, beamed ceiling and doors that pull closed when needed.

Draftsmen, gathered under the double-height ceiling, enjoy natural light from above and from the surrounding windows.

The private office contains the bare essentials: open storage for reference materials and plentiful work surfaces. The steel beam is one of the many unexpected details that delight the eye and lift the spirit.

Presentations are made in the spacious mezzanine with its ample skylight windows.

Photographs: Laura Salvati

The Rural...

ARCHITECTS: Hawkweed

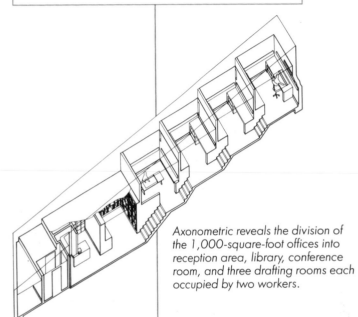

Axonometric reveals the division of the 1,000-square-foot offices into reception area, library, conference room, and three drafting rooms each occupied by two workers.

Sun visors over the windows control the heat gain while allowing in the light.

The passive solar building follows the upward slope of a south-facing hillside.

Like the wildflower that gave them their name, the Hawkweed group of architects of Osseo, Wisconsin, designed an office building for themselves that responds to the sun. Located on a wooded farmland, near their homes, the six-person office is almost totally lit and heated by the sun.

The architects' use of the land reveals the importance of siting in passive-solar building, their specialty. Notched into a slope of land, the building faces south, receiving the sun through its large, well-insulated, visored windows. Inside, enough light is reflected from the white walls for comfortable working so that only rarely are the back-up fluorescent lamps needed. In addition to helping distribute the light, the flat ceiling also holds down the volume that needs to be heated. On winter mornings, the sun's thin heat is supplemented by a wood-burning stove that uses up the office trash. In the summer, the open windows circulate the air in the upward-sloping, narrow (14 ft. deep) space. This harmonious coexistence with nature is not a nostalgic return to a romantic rural life, but an alternative to the larger business world, which can insert itself through the telephone, parcel service, and land or air transportation.

...The Urban

ARCHITECTS: Rivkin/Weisman

The conference room is equipped with slide-projection facilities and an ever-changing streetscape.

Workers in the drafting room are aware of activity beyond the glass-block wall, in the adjoining conference room, but the movement is never specific enough to be distracting.

The curved front of the Rockefeller apartments, opposite New York's Museum of Modern Art, dictated the plan of the Rivkin/Weisman architecture offices. A door, niched into the building's façade, opens from the street into a layer of public spaces: the reception is angled into one bay, the conference room into the other.

While light from the windows is brought into the main offices through glass-block walls, the distracting movement of city traffic is obscured by the same. The two large drafting rooms, each shared by four people, are thus given visual and acoustic privacy from their urban surrounding. With the pleasant lighting, recessed floors, and large work surfaces, these two centers of activity—joined by a connecting corridor in the back—were designed to promote interchange between people working on the same project, whether that be a bank interior or an addition to the city skyline.

Photographs: Dan Cornish

Sensitive Restorers

DESIGNER: Rita St. Clair

While others reinvent past styles, Rita St. Clair restores them. In the process, she creates interiors that have the richness and charm of a more leisurely time combined with the comfort and efficiency we've grown to expect. Her well-known and recognized ability in the renovation and adaptive re-use of interiors is beautifully illustrated in the branch office she set up for her growing business.

In an 1830s New York townhouse, the new office can function as an autonomous workplace for the visiting principal and her resident associate, while in close communication with the 18-member home office in Baltimore. So, the need for storage of samples, catalogs, working drawings, bookkeeping is kept to a minimum, while the atmosphere of comfort and elegance is emphasized for the benefit of new clients.

Only about one-third of the space is taken up by the built-in work surfaces. The rest of the floor contains a reception/sitting area, a conference room where civilized breakfasts and luncheons are often served, a kitchen, a bath, and a small bedroom.

The extensive renovation work that went into this decep-

tively simple space included totally gutting a room, opening up doors where there were none, closing up two fireplaces and reactivating another, installing new plumbing and wiring, repairing and replacing the plasterwork, woodwork, and the etched glass. The worn floors are covered in a tight-weave commercial-grade carpet; the irregular walls are hidden under a flame-proofed fabric that is edged with chrome strips. This neutral setting was planned to receive a new set of antiques, accessories, and artwork as Mrs. St. Clair's clients purchase the existing decorations.

The long, narrow work tops with rounded corners, installed atop lateral files, provide the needed space for spreading out the tools of the interior design trade: samples of fabric, wallpaper, tiles; photographs of furniture; and large drawings of plans and sections.

Set up like a comfortable living room, the reception/sitting area is a prelude to the conference room beyond the etched-glass doors.

Photographs: Peter Paige

Material Innovator

DESIGNER: Kevin Walz

At the front door, the reception/ waiting area is furnished with a built-in banquette with baglike pillows attached as backrests. The facing fiberglass wall shares the light but not the sound of the office next door.

Although their loft was large and it comfortably combined the living and working needs of designer Kevin Walz and his photographer wife Barbara Walz, when their respective businesses grew and their baby came, someone had to move. So Kevin relocated his studio in a pre-war building on New York City's lower Fifth Avenue.

Known for his innovative use of interesting materials, Walz built the walls of his new offices from the inexpensive fiberglass that's used for skylights. Easy to cut and install, this material consists of two translucent sheets strengthened by aluminum frames, which form either linear or square patterns. The sheets sandwich a thick layer of air between them, stopping sounds from coming through, yet letting in light.

Walz Designs is set up as a series of enclosed offices for the receptionist, the principal, and two drafters. While only the designer's work space has doors, the other areas are made private by the right-angled, high walls that stop short of the eleven-foot ceilings.

The designer's office contains a high counter where he can work standing or perched on a high stool. The counter's fold-down top accommodates oversize drawings. A built-in storage unit with its own, wide work surface lines the wall behind.

Photographs: Thomas Hooper

In the Country

An old three-level farmhouse has been restored and converted to a workplace and home by stage designer Andre Benaim for himself. Traces of his work are found in the prototype rockers that have appeared in a Strindberg play as well as models of sets being built.

If creative work can be compartmentalized at all, Benaim's takes place in a former cellar that has a separate entrance through a French door from the garden. Here the nondistracting interior views and a welcome access to nature give him the space to dream. But the house is only a short distance from Florence, so the city's active life is frequently brought into the private workplace.

The workroom's double-decker floor allows for a convenient separation between the dining area, set up on the upper level adjacent to the kitchen, and the work table, which has an evocative view of a prosceniumlike arch. The obliquely cut stairwell leads to the upstairs bedrooms and baths.

The subtle drama of the spare space is enhanced by the red striping that highlights the beams and the uneven wood-grain pattern of the floor, which is made of strips taken from old casks and vats found in this former cellar.

The simple façade of this Italian farmhouse reveals the organization of its rooms. Each room is centered about an opening to the outdoors, each room secluded from its neighbor by a door. This arrangement is as well suited to the current lifestyles of a writer/producer and a fashion stylist, as it had been for generations of farming families.

The two studies, one in a corner room, one slightly off center, are separated from each other by a large kitchen/dining room. Each work space has an exterior view that looks out to the surrounding orchards. For the writer, this environment serves as a reminder of the passage of time on nature's everchanging face.

In the City

ARCHITECT:
Billie Tsien
of
Tod Williams and Associates

The living room is centered on a dhurrie rug that picks up the pastel colors of the walls and trimmings. The studio's mysterious window gives a center to this spacious room, beyond which the artist's work-in-progress can be glimpsed.

One of the difficulties of living and working in the same place is separating the two when necessary. For illustrator Cathy Barancik, this has been solved by a series of walls that identify each area in her New York loft. The walls work much like the façades of the buildings along the city street—establishing the separateness *and* relatedness of each unit to the whole.

When the artist goes to work, day or night, she literally crosses the "street" from the "building" that's her bedroom to the "building" that's her office. The front door of the bedroom unit opens to a hallway that functions like an arcade; the artist can cross the arcade to the front door of the studio, which can also be entered from the open space that joins it to the living/reception area.

The separate entity of the studio is emphasized by the full-height wall whose window fronts the living room. On the other side the studio houses a storage wall and an assistant's work surface, a large table, a rolling credenza, and a stepladder. The artist's work surface is the wall to which the large illustrations are pinned.

Barancik's familiar style, seen in many magazines, takes shape on large sheets of paper pinned to the studio's wall.

The many photographs, fabrics, and other objects that the artist needs as references for her work are filed in the built-in storage area where an assistant can gather visual materials necessary for each project.

Photographs: Langdon Clay

Return to Nature

An artist and a physicist might seem an unlikely pair. But remembering that both do a great deal of thinking and experimenting for the sake of finding "elegant" solutions to problems, the two professions might well be seen as two different branches of aesthetics.

The pair in this case live and work in a restored farmhouse in the Tuscany region of Italy. The artist does her large, ethereal paintings on the upper level of a shared studio, which was once used to salt salami. The physicist works with his personal computer, calculator, typewriter, technical manuals, and model heating pipes in the lower level of the same room, which was formerly a stable. The two spread their work throughout the house and gardens; they refer to the various projects as "pieces of thoughts."

Photograph: Silvio Wolf/Abitare

Scientists at Cold Spring Harbor Laboratory, on the north shore of Long Island in New York, work on an 80-acre complex of 19 buildings that resemble a century-old fishing village. This rural scientific enclave reflects the attitude of its director, James D. Watson, one of the three men who received the Nobel Prize for discovering the structure of DNA. In opposition to the pristine isolation of many modern research centers, Watson believes that the best scientific work occurs in informal settings where researchers are never far from the reality of nature whose micro-forms they isolate in their labs.

The Neurology Lab (partial view), housed in a charming 1892 shingled building, is a highly specialized workplace where scientists are implanting micro-electrodes into the nerve cells of leeches. Because the experiments are extremely sensitive to the light conditions, temperature changes, any kind of movement, and any electrical interference, four separate labs were constructed (axonometric). Each has its own climate and light control; each is protected from movement and electronic interference by concrete slab floors and grounded aluminum skins. The chairs grouped around the fireplace bring workers together for idea exchanges during the casual chats that relieve their isolated work.

ARCHITECTS: Moore Grover Harper

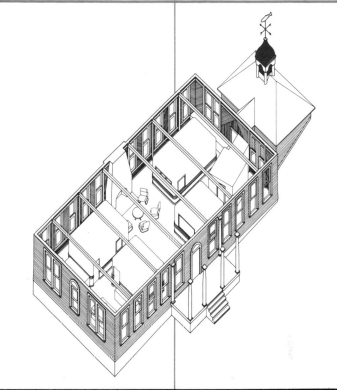

Photograph: Norman McGrath

Bill Blass

ARCHITECTS:
Wayne Berg
and
Richard Weinstein

The creative nature of the designer as artist is expressed in the placement of Bill Blass' private office in the 10,000-square-foot New York showroom/offices of the company that bears his name. Twisted away from the Seventh Avenue views, the executive office breaks the architectural grid of the surrounding areas that house the dressmakers, tailors, and support staff. Also breaking the grid are two private offices occupied by Blass' two key people: the assistant designer and the publicity manager.

Blass' private office stands alone as a country house in its garden. The harsh city light that rushes through the building's windows becomes dappled as it falls into the living-room-like office through the foliage that guards the French windows.

Bill Blass' favorite place is his country house. His city office duplicates that feeling in its bleached wood floor, travertine desk, linen walls and upholstery, and large windows.

The offices of the two key assistants are basically two open cubes that are angled to protect the privacy of each. The interior walls are lined with a soft material on which current work is pinned up. The separateness of these offices from their surroundings is emphasized by their overhead grid, which filters the ceiling's general fluorescent light and casts a halo above the cubicles.

Photographs: Paul Warchol

L'Zinger

ARCHITECT:
Billie Tsien
of
Tod Williams
and
Associates

A serene Japanese house that rises discreetly from its surrounding gardens is recalled in the design of the L'Zinger showroom. Located in one of New York's busiest fashion buildings on Seventh Avenue, this peaceful environment is sensitively tuned to the line of graceful clothing sold here.

Basically used as a selling space, the showroom is orga-nized around an enclosable conference room. Phone sales go on in the back room, while buyers are hosted in the large, open area that's fronted by the "porch" of the conference room. The clothes that are shown here are placed on red wooden screens, which when not in use, are distributed throughout the space as delicate monuments to the merchandise.

At the entrance, Billie Tsien's large, abstract sculpture of a solid concrete block with a sheet of copper sliced into it, blocks direct access to the showroom. Much like a big stone in a Japanese garden, the sculpture requires visitors to walk around it. The three different materials used on the floors mark the transition of one space into another: The vinyl tile in the showroom area changes to slate tile at the conference room entrance, which changes to precast concrete panels with maple insets inside the conference room.

Photographs: Langdon Clay

Inside the conference room, a high-gloss table and chairs are centered under the coffered ceiling with its cool-toned, recessed fluorescent light.

The conference room, with its shoji-screen walls and sliding door made of etched glass and ebonized oak, becomes a dramatic point in the runway twice a year when L'Zinger holds its fashion shows. At other times, it hosts staff meetings.

Glamour Merchants

The glass walls that separate the main showroom from the enclosed sales offices at Private Eyes Sunglass Corp., in New York City, serve a double purpose: They cut down the noise of several sales conversations going on at once; at the same time they provide a generous overview of the interior and its contents.
INTERIOR DESIGN: Kurland Silvester

A New York diamond wholesaler and his son conduct their highly specialized transactions over an L-shaped partners' desk. The gems are passed back and forth with tweezers over the white desk pads and weighed on the sensitive digital scales. The jewelers' lamps (double stemmed for use by both the buyer and the seller) allow for close examination of the diamonds. The offices are secured by a buzzer mechanism that automatically locks the doors of the showroom and the adjacent factory-workroom when the front doors open.
INTERIOR DESIGN: Inscape

A recent renovation at Damon Creations, a New York menswear company, has resulted in a new way of giving private showings to three separate buyers at one time. A row of three, 23-foot-long cabinets each containing Damon's complete line, is arranged facing a long window wall. The curved exteriors of these cabinets follow the shape of the table inside the showrooms where merchandise is spread out around the buyer, who sits at the center. The three showrooms have no doors, but a recessed entrance defined by a glass-block dividing wall and the cabinet which ensure visual privacy during showings. At each end of the curved desk, an assistant keeps the records. The merchandise's correct color is seen under the fluorescent uplights which are supplemented by incandescent downlights and daylight from the windows.
ARCHITECT: Wayne Berg

Photograph: Wayne Berg (bottom)

Photograph: Stuart Davis (top)

Attorneys

ARCHITECTS:
Salvati Tresoldi

The offices for a group of attorneys in Milan are located in that city's famous Galleria. The grand views of the Galleria's arcade are brought inside through the windows incised into the historic building's stones. The plain geometry that announces itself at the reception area is repeated in the form of the furnishings, which are reminiscent of the color compositions of Piet Mondrian. These delightful references to the times that gave the present its unique character are also emphasized at the law library's entrance. Here, nineteenth-century virtuosity combines with twentieth-century abstraction in a fanciful composition of painted canvas that's rigged across the ceiling and to chunks of walls, sailing into the legal imagination.

The Galleria is seen through the arched window of the hallway that is separated from the offices by a glass wall.

Serious study and research are preceded by a delightful rush of color and texture in the free-form sculpture of the law library.

Each office is made unique by the color combination of the shelving, the placement of the boxy filing cabinet, and the architectural detailing. Here, one of the corners ripples like an accordion.

Photographs: Laura Salvati

Obstetrician/Gynecologist

ARCHITECT: Robert A.M. Stern

Women who have put off having children are joining their more youthful sisters in obstetric/gynecologic offices. The architecture of one growing group practice in New York gives a heroic scale to what might indeed be the grandest adventure in human life. But even those entrants who are less vitally involved can read the procession of pilasters, beams, and soft light from keystonelike lamps as signs of a civilized place where one can expect to be treated well. The reassuring quality of the office, in addition to its calm symmetry, is underscored by its delicate pastel colors: cool in the public spaces of the reception area, waiting room, and hall; warm in the consultation rooms and in the examining rooms where it softens somewhat the severe, clinical atmosphere set by high-technology.

The reception and record keeping functions are enclosed in a central room, its front window parapet repeating the form of the entry hall.

The symmetrically furnished waiting room resembles a cozy, softly lit living room that makes for easy social interaction between the women.

The consulting rooms that are the physicians' private offices are small desk-and-chair arrangements painted a warm, creamy, "dignified" color.

The library/conference room for the physicians is painted the same soft pink as the examining rooms. Clinical views of X-rays on one wall alternate with a witty painting of the same subject on the other wall.

Photographs: E. Stoecklein

The view from the wood-paneled waiting room, where patients fill out forms at the curving corner-desk, reveals the diagonal flow of space directed by the metal-faced, black-top reception desk. The wall of the first examining room along this corridor is a sea-foam green.

Generalists and Specialists

An addition of 800 square feet to a New York gastro-intestinal specialists' office provided the opportunity to reorganize the flow of increased traffic, create a series of highly private examining rooms, and expand the administrative area's work and filing capabilities. These changes were accomplished by architects of the Design Collaborative by building a diagonally placed reception/administrative area with curves that undulate through the center of the space, providing a strong direction that is reinforced by the straight line of the recessed ceiling lights. The former, busy reception area at right angles to the entrance was turned into a comfortable waiting room, now niched in a protected corner. Its homey feeling is conveyed through the mellow, wood-panelled walls, coffered ceilings (both existing architectural details), and the new, leather club chairs, wall sconces, and table lamps.

In the room where highly private matters become the subject of clinical study, the cold lights and scrubbed surfaces convert both the examiner and the examined into objective observers of symptoms.

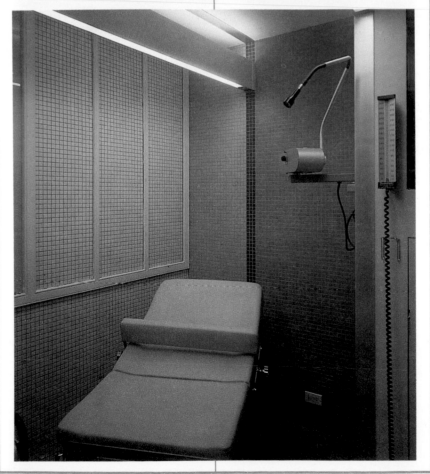

The promise of considerate and competent treatment is conveyed by architect Steven Levine with Laverne Dagras in the waiting room of the SoHo Medical Group in lower Manhattan. The large area that spans the width of this former industrial loft is arranged like a front parlor where seating for quiet conversations, solitary reverie, and private correspondence are arranged in safe distances from one another. Because their patients come from all age groups, a separate area for the more active younger set is niched into the corner of the waiting room, nearby parents and the nurses at the adjacent reception desk.

The noises and movements of the public rooms are blocked from the interior offices with the help of angled walls. The beam that spans the reception desk continues on to form the brow of the entrance to the doctors' work area. The diagonal wall of the children's waiting room, stepped-up wall of the reception area, and beam all funnel traffic into the examination rooms.

At the end of the long hall, the three doctors' offices, equal in size and furnishings, are perceived as a wall of glass. Actually, the translucent surface that forms the curved wall of the central office only, is meant to bring daylight into the corridor from the private office's skylight. The doors to these offices are hidden in niches to discourage anyone from entering who is not specifically invited there.

The center office, one of the three private consulting rooms at the end of the hall, has a curved glass-block wall, topped by a clerestory. Both the placement and the texture of the materials guard the visual and acoustic privacy of the room while sharing the light and architectural texture of the spaces beyond.

Indications of the space beyond the waiting room are given by the open pressed-tin ceiling and a view of the interior hall with its strong pattern of columns and soft, glass-block filtered light. But the traffic within is hidden from view by the angles of the walls.

Photographs: Norman McGrath

Home Practice

ARCHITECT: Charles Boxenbaum

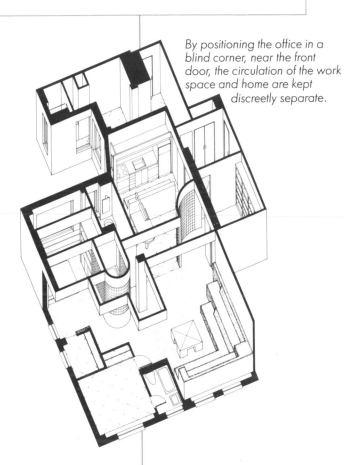

By positioning the office in a blind corner, near the front door, the circulation of the work space and home are kept discreetly separate.

In the West Side office of a New York psychologist, a patient is completely unaware of the home beyond the private room where the consultation is taking place. Niched into a windowless, inside corner, the office has its own entrance from the hall. It is kept apart from the rest of the apartment by the bi-fold doors that close up the curved glass-block wall and by the venetian blinds of the interior window. During one-on-one sessions, the glass surfaces bring in reassuring daylight from the apartment's windows, while containing the room's thoughts and sounds within. When the doctor is at his solitary work, his office can become part of the household when he opens the doors and blinds. The only time that the office takes over part of the home is during those times that group sessions congregate on the living room's stepped-up, padded platforms.

Floor plan courtesy Charles Boxenbaum

The office is a simply furnished room with a wall of books behind the desk and a wall of glass that closes it in for complete privacy.

The open plan of the apartment is not without a strong definition of space. The half-wall of the food-preparation area keeps it separated from the attached dining room. The change of flooring from tile to carpet marks the passage into the living room and its private corner office.

Photograph: Norman McGrath

At Home Study

ARCHITECT: Emilio Ambasz

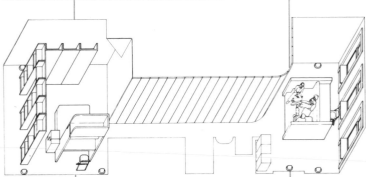

The hall that separates the sitting/desk area from the bedroom/study contains a row of rooms, including a bar, several storage spaces, a bath, and a dressing room. The bed's top perch can be reached by the carpeted steps that fold into a cubelike table when no one wants to dream in the heights. There's an additional work surface built into the back of the bed's colossal headboard.

A life in art, with its constant surges of "aesthetic emotion," seems to yearn for silent, contemplative times when the world of the museum and gallery is left behind. For art collector Barbara Jakobsen, this need for solitude became especially urgent as she began to furnish her New York townhouse with significant designs of the 1940s and 1950s, including those of Noguchi, Risom, and Eames. In contrast to the sunny

downstairs rooms made for conversations, the upstairs hideaway is a place to do quiet paperwork and research or for private moments with family.

The two rooms at either end of the upper floor combine a study and bedroom. The large desk/sofa combination that dominates the front room is seen by its owner as a "monumental minimalist sculpture in an urban park." The bedroom's own monumental sculptures are

a colonnade of bookshelves that present a blank face to the bed which, in itself, serves as a desk, high-perch, and the usual sleeping surface. Velvet walls, a mysterious uplight from the turtlelike fixtures that line up along the floor, touchable carpet and furniture surfaces make this a highly sensual environment without the obvious visual stimulations. Here the "landscape of the mind" ranges over an unobstructed view.

Floor plan courtesy Emilio Ambasz

A colonnade of bookshelves, faces turned toward the window, screens out the views while allowing light into the bedroom.

A single piece of furniture combines the double functions of work surface and lounge.

Photographs: Norman McGrath

Glassed-In Retreats

Solitude and connectedness are admirably combined in this study built into the attic of a Milan house. Hidden among the rooftops of the city, removed from the rest of the household by a spiral staircase that leads to the living room and the spacious terrace below, the study is an ideal place for quiet work. Oak shelves line the perimeter walls. Conforming to their continuous line is a desk niched into a corner, facing a small, dense, roof garden. Other shelves are suspended from the ceiling or divide the room into two different sections—one area defined by an Oriental rug, the other by a modern design—each in aesthetic harmony with the polished brick floor. The soft, linen shades can close out the sharp rays and heat of the sun, but not its light.

ARCHITECT: Rosanna Monzoni

Photographs: Gabriele Basilico

A greenhouse, open to the lower Manhattan panorama, was adapted as a study for a film director. The small interior space seems larger than it is because the bleached decking is used as a continuous surfacing material: from the deep wall of shelves to the platform seating and the floor that continue outside on the open terrace. This unity of material and color adds to the visual space of the room as does the mirrored upper portion of the plank walls that reflect an infinity of metal frames. As throughout the duplex penthouse, the few furnishings are carefully selected. The tawny blond finishes of the greenhouse study become a rich, red-brown in the adjacent dining room, which is in a clear stylistic relationship with the study.
ARCHITECTS: Shelton, Storz, Mindel

Photographs: Bo Parker

Libraries

This surburban New Jersey family of five has the good fortune of owning a room where knowlege is stored and waiting for those who seek it—their library. The process is made pleasant by the many amenities we have come to associate with good, home libraries: a closed door, wraparound shelves of books, comfortable seating and lounges, pools of warm light available at every reading nook, a glowing fireplace, openings with clear views of the outdoors and slightly abstracted views of the surrounding rooms, and a commodious desk with a luxuriously smooth writing top. The restful gray-green colors, the classically inspired desk, window pediment, and moldings—a reassuring symmetry in the architecture—all work to welcome the seeker of knowledge.
ARCHITECT: Robert A. M. Stern

A library of another kind holds its information in the electronic impulses that light up three television screens, a VCR, and digital read-outs of time and temperature in two cities. The equipment is built flush with the front of the burgundy lacquer cabinet, maintaining the smooth-surfaced calmness of the room. Such a showcase of home electronics would not be complete without the sensor in the floor that turns on the lights when someone enters the room. The lighting fixtures, built into the top and bottom of the cantilevered storage cabinet, can be adjusted in intensity. The area dominated by the burgundy-leather desk, designed originally for Cartier, has a wood floor to allow the easy roll of chair casters. A change from the hard, working area to soft seating at the chaise that is niched into the end of the room, is underscored by the velvet carpet. The quiet luxury of today's electronically sophisticated home office is contained inside gray, flannel-covered walls.

DESIGNERS: Bromley/Jacobsen

Useful Addresses

Architects and Designers: United States

EMILIO AMBASZ
207 East 32nd Street
New York, New York 10001

BARKER, RINKER, SEACAT & PARTNERS
2546 15th Street
Denver, Colorado 80211

WAYNE BERG ARCHITECT
1133 Broadway
New York, New York 10010

CHARLES BOXENBAUM ARCHITECT
1860 Broadway
New York, New York 10023

BROMLEY & JACOBSEN ARCHITECTURE AND DESIGN
242 West 27th Street
New York, New York 10010

SAMUEL J. DESANTO ARCHITECT
140 West 57th Street
New York, New York 10019

DESIGN COLLABORATIVE
140 West 57th Street
New York, New York 10019

ENVIRONMENTAL PLANNING & RESEARCH
1000 Potomac Street, N.W.
Washington, D.C. 20037

JOYCE FRONEY J.R. STRINGANO ARCHITECTURE & DESIGN
300 East 59th Street
New York, New York 10022

ARTHUR GENSLER & ASSOCIATES
823 UN Plaza
New York, New York 10017

Regional Offices:

633 17th Street
Suite 1220
Denver, Colorado 80202

700 Rusk Street
Houston, Texas 77002

2049 Century Park East
Suite 570
Los Angeles, California 90067

550 Kearny Street
9th Floor
San Francisco, California 94103

GWATHMEY SIEGEL ASSOCIATES
475 10th Avenue
New York, New York 10018

HAMBRECHT TERRELL INTERNATIONAL
860 Broadway
New York, New York 10003

THE HAWKWEED GROUP LTD.
Route 4, Box 175A
Osseo, Wisconsin 54758

ISD INCORPORATED
305 East 46th Street
New York, New York 10017

Regional Offices:

400 North State Street
Chicago, Illinois 60610

1900 Wazee Street
Denver, Colorado 80202

2 Shell Plaza
Houston, Texas 77002

INSCAPE INTERIOR DESIGNS INC.
40 East 88th Street
New York, New York 10028

KURLAND SILVESTER DESIGN INC.
232 Madison Avenue
New York, New York 10016

STEPHEN LEVINE ARCHITECTS
1133 Broadway
New York, New York 10010

THE MILLER ORGANIZATION
149 Madison Avenue
New York, New York 10016

MOORE GROVER HARPER
P.O. Box 409
Essex, Connecticut 06426

NEVILLE LEWIS ASSOCIATES, INC.
141 East 8th Street
New York, New York 10003

Regional Offices:

1910 Pacific Avenue
Dallas, Texas 75201

1624 Market Street
Denver, Colorado 80202

437 Grant Street
Pittsburgh, Pennsylvania 15219

1111 Third Avenue
Seattle, Washington 98101

SANDRA NUNNERLEY
Interior Design
400 East 55th Street
New York, New York 10022

CHRISTOPHER H.L. OWEN, AIA
330 East 59th Street
New York, New York 10022

KENNETH PARKER ASSOCIATES
411 North 20th Street
Philadelphia, Pennsylvania 19130

POWELL/KLEINSCHMIDT
115 South La Salle
Chicago, Illinois 60603

RITA ST. CLAIR ASSOCIATES
LTD.
1009 North Charles Street
Baltimore, Maryland 21201

Regional Offices:

127 East 10th Street
New York, New York 10003

RIVKIN/WEISMAN P.C.
ARCHITECTS
17 West 54th Street
New York, New York 10022

SHELTON STORZ MINDEL
ARCHITECTS
216 West 18th Street
Penthouse Suite
New York, New York 10011

SPACE DESIGN GROUP
8 West 40th Street
New York, New York 10018

ROBERT A.M. STERN
ARCHITECT
200 West 72nd Street
New York, New York 10023

J.R. STRIGNANO,
ARCHITECTURE AND DESIGN
300 East 59th Street
New York, New York 10022

CHARLES SWERZ &
ASSOCIATES
202 West 40th Street
New York, New York 10018

BILLIE TSIEN
TOD WILLIAMS AND
ASSOCIATES
222 Central Park South
New York, New York 10020

VOORSANGER & MILLS
ASSOCIATES
30 West 57th Street
New York, New York 10019

WALZ DESIGNS
8 West 40th Street
New York, New York 10018

Architects and Designers: Italy

ASCARELLI, MACCIOCCHI,
NICOLAO, PARISIO
Via Guilia 163
00186 Rome

SLAVATI TRESOLDI
ARCHITECTS
Piazza Borromeo 10
20123 Milan

Associations: United States

ACOUSTICAL SOCIETY OF
AMERICA
335 East 45th Street
New York, New York 10017

ADMINISTRATIVE
MANAGEMENT SOCIETY
Maryland Road
Willow Grow, Pennsylvania 19090

AMERICAN INSTITUTE OF
ARCHITECTS
1735 New York Avenue, N.W.
Washington, D.C. 20006

AMERICAN INSTITUTE OF
MANAGEMENT
125 East 38th Street
New York, New York 10016

AMERICAN MANAGEMENT
ASSOCIATION
135 West 50th Street
New York, New York 10020

AMERICAN SOCIETY OF CIVIL
ENGINEERS
345 East 47th Street
New York, New York 10017

AMERICAN SOCIETY FOR
INDUSTRIAL SECURITY
2000 K Street, N.W.
Washington, D.C. 20006

AMERICAN SOCIETY OF
INTERIOR DESIGNERS
730 Fifth Avenue
New York, New York 10019

ART DEALERS ASSOCIATION
OF AMERICA
575 Madison Avenue
New York, New York 10022

ASSOCIATION OF RECORDS
MANAGERS AND
ADMINISTRATION
P.O. Box 281
Bradford, Rhode Island 02808

AUDIO ENGINEERING SOCIETY
60 East 42nd Street
New York, New York 10017

BIFMA (THE BUSINESS AND
INSTITUTIONAL FURNITURE
MANUFACTURERS
ASSOCIATION)
2335 Burton, S.E.
Grand Rapids, Michigan 49506

BUILDING OWNERS AND
MANAGERS ASSOCIATION
1221 Massachusetts Avenue, N.W.
Washington, D.C. 20005

CARPET AND RUG INSTITUTE
P.O. Box 2048
Dalton, Georgia 30720

CERAMIC TILE INSTITUTE
700 North Virgil Street
Los Angeles, California 90029

DESIGN MANAGEMENT
INSTITUTE
Massachusetts College of Art
50 Milk Street, 15th Floor
Boston, Massachusetts 02109

ENVIRONMENTAL DESIGN
RESEARCH ASSOCIATION, INC.
L'Enfant Plaza Station
P.O. Box 23129
Washington, D.C. 20024

FACILITIES MANAGEMENT
INSTITUTE
3971 South Research Park Drive
Ann Arbor, Michigan 48104

ILLUMINATING ENGINEERING
SOCIETY
345 East 47th Street
New York, New York 10017

INDUSTRIAL DESIGNERS
SOCIETY OF AMERICA
1750 Old Meadow Road
McLean, Virginia 22101

INSTITUTE OF BUSINESS
DESIGNERS
1155 Merchandise Mart
Chicago, Illinois 60654

INSTITUTE OF ELECTRICAL
AND ELECTRONICS ENGINEERS
345 East 47th Street
New York, New York 10017

INSTITUTE OF MANAGEMENT
CONSULTANTS
347 Madison Avenue
New York, New York 10017

INSTITUTE FOR PROFESSIONAL
EDUCATION
1901 North Fort Myer Drive
Arlington, Virginia 22209

INTERIOR PLANTSCAPE
ASSOCIATION
11800 Sunrise Valley Drive
Reston, Virginia 22091

INTERNATIONAL AUDIOVISUAL
SOCIETY
P.O. Box 54
Cullowhee, North Carolina 28723

NATIONAL COUNCIL OF
ACOUSTICAL CONSULTANTS
8811 Colesville Road
Silver Spring, Maryland 20910

NATIONAL FIRE PREVENTION
ASSOCIATION
470 Atlantic Avenue
Boston, Massachusetts 02110

NATIONAL RECORDS
MANAGEMENT COUNCIL
60 East 42nd Street
New York, New York 10017

SOCIETY OF PROFESSIONAL
MANAGEMENT CONSULTANTS
205 West 89th Street
New York, New York 10024

TILE COUNCIL OF AMERICA,
INC.
P.O. Box 2222
Princeton, New Jersey 08540

WOMEN'S OCCUPATIONAL
HEALTH RESOURCE CENTER
Columbia University School of Public
Health
60 Haven Avenue B-1
New York, New York 10032

Associations: United Kingdom

BRITISH INSTITUTE OF
INTERIOR DESIGN
22–24 South Street
Ilkeston, Derbyshire

FURNITURE INDUSTRY
RESEARCH ASSOCIATION
Maxwell Road
Stevenage, Hertfordshire

OFFICE MACHINES AND
EQUIPMENT FEDERATION
16 Wood Street
Kingston-upon-Thames KT1 1VE

BRITISH FURNITURE
MANUFACTURERS' FEDERATED
ASSOCIATIONS
30 Harcourt Street
London W1H 2AA

SIAD (SOCIETY OF INDUSTRIAL
ARTISTS AND DESIGNERS)
12 Carlton House Terrace
London SW1

THE DESIGN COUNCIL
28 Haymarket
London SW1Y 4SU

RIBA (ROYAL INSTITUTE OF
BRITISH ARCHITECTS)
66 Portland Place
London W1

Associations: Australia, Japan, New Zealand, South Africa

BRANZ (BUILDING RESEARCH
ASSOCIATION OF NEW
ZEALAND)
P.O. Box 9375
Wellington

DESIGN INSTITUTE SOUTH
AFRICAN BUREAU OF
STANDARDS
H5 22 Forum Building
Stuben Street
Private Bag X191
Pretoria 0001
Transvaal

IDCA (INDUSTRIAL DESIGN
COUNCIL OF AUSTRALIA)
The National Secretariat
114 Williams Street
Melbourne, Victoria 3000

IDEA (INDUSTRIAL DESIGN
INSTITUTE OF AUSTRALIA)
21 Burwood Road, 2nd Floor
Hawthorn, Victoria 3122

INSTITUTE OF SOUTH
AFRICAN ARCHITECTS and
SOUTH AFRICAN COUNCIL FOR
ARCHITECTS
P.O. Box 31756
Braamfomtein, 2017

JAPAN ARCHITECTS
ASSOCIATION
Kenchiku-ka Kaikan
Sibuya-ku
2-3-16 Jingumae
Tokyo

NEW ZEALAND INDUSTRIAL
DESIGN COUNCIL
70 Ghuzmee Street
Wellington
(Postal Private Bag Tearo)

NEW ZEALAND INSTITUTE OF
ARCHITECTS
Maritime Branch
2-10 Custom House K
Wellington

NEW ZEALAND SOCIETY OF
INDUSTRIAL DESIGNERS
P.O. Box 3432
Auckland

ROYAL AUSTRALIAN
INSTITUTE OF ARCHITECTS
2A Mugga Way
Redhill, Act 2603

SOCIETY OF INDUSTRIAL
ARTISTS AND DESIGNERS OF
SOUTH AFRICA
National Council
P.O. Box 23394
Jobert Park 2044
Transvaal

Sources: *Carpeting*

BRINTON'S CARPETS USA LTD.
913 Third Avenue
New York, New York 10022

LEES CARPETS
Valley Forge Corporate Center
King of Prussia, Pennsylvania 19406

PATCRAFT MILLS INC.
913 Third Avenue
New York, New York 10022

ROSECORE CARPET
979 Third Avenue
New York, New York 10022

STARK CARPET
979 Third Avenue
New York, New York 10022

V'SOSKE INC. CARPET
155 East 56th Street
New York, New York 10022

Sources:
Fabrics

BRUNSCHWIG & FILS, INC.
410 East 62nd Street
New York, New York 10021

GRETCHEN BELLINGER, INC.
979 Third Avenue
New York, New York 10022

BRICKEL ASSOCIATES, INC.
515 Madison Avenue
New York, New York 10022

DONGHIA FABRICS
979 Third Avenue
New York, New York 10022

JACK LENOR LARSEN
41 East 11th Street
New York, New York 10003

LEE JOFA
979 Third Avenue
New York, New York 10022

BORIS KROLL
979 Third Avenue
New York, New York 10022

SUNAR LTD.
18 Marshall Street
Norwalk, Connecticut 06584

Sources:
Furniture

ATELIER INTERNATIONAL
LTD.
595 Madison Avenue
New York, New York 10022

BAKER FURNITURE
No. 914 Merchandise Mart
Chicago, Illinois 60654

BENEDETTI
3011 East Pico Boulevard
Los Angeles, California 90023

BRAYTON INTERNATIONAL
150 East 58th Street
New York, New York 10022

BRICKEL ASSOCIATES, INC.
515 Madison Avenue
New York, New York 10022

BRUETON INDUSTRIES, INC.
227-02 145 Road
Springfield Gardens, New York 11413

DUNBAR FURNITURE CORP.
601 South Fulton Street
Berne, Indiana 46711

HERMAN MILLER INC.
8500 Byron Road
Zeeland, Michigan 49464

HARVEY PROBBER INC.
44 Probber Lane
Fall River, Massachusetts 02726

INTERNATIONAL CONTRACT
FURNISHERS (ICF)
305 East 63rd Street
New York, New York 10021

INTREX
341 East 62nd Street
New York, New York 10021

KNOLL INTERNATIONAL
655 Madison Avenue
New York, New York 10021

KINETICS
150 East 58th Street
New York, New York 10022

KRUEGER
1330 Bellevue Street, P.O. Box 8100
Green Bay, Wisconsin 54308

STEELCASE INC.
1120 36th Street, S.E.
Grand Rapids, Michigan 49501

SUNAR, LTD.
18 Marshall Street
Norwalk, Connecticut 06584

THONET INDUSTRIES
491 East Princess Street, P.O. Box
1587
York, Pennsylvania 17405

VECTA CONTRACT, INC.
1800 South Great Southwest Parkway
Grand Prairie, Texas 75051

WOOD & HOGAN
305 East 63rd Street
New York, New York 10021

ZOGRAPHOS DESIGNS LTD.
150 East 58th Street
New York, New York 10022

Sources:
Lighting

ARTEMIDE INC.
150 East 58th Street
New York, New York 10022

CHAPMAN LAMPS FURNITURE
& ACCESSORIES
21 East 26th Street
New York, New York 10010

HABITAT, INC.
150 East 58th Street
New York, New York 10022

LIGHTOLIER INC.
346 Claremont Avenue
Jersey City, New Jersey 07305

NESSEN LAMPS, INC.
3200 Jerome Avenue
Bronx, New York 10468

RAMBUSCH
40 West 13th Street
New York, New York 10011

Bibliography

Altman, Irwin. *The Environment and Social Behavior.* Belmont, California: Wadsworth Publishing Co., 1975.

"Arranging the Model Office." *World's Work*, Vol. X, 1905.

Deal, Terrence E. and Allan A. Kennedy. *Corporate Cultures.* Reading, Massachusetts: Addison-Wesley Publishing Co., 1982.

Drucker, Stephen. "Home as Office: Mergers that Work." *The New York Times*, HOME Section, March 31, 1983.

Goodrich, Ronald J. "Human Logic in the Office of the Future." Speech delivered at Information Management Conference, New York. October 11–14, 1982.

_____. "Seven Evaluations: A Review." Reprint from *Environment and Behavior.* Beverly Hills and London: Sage Publications.

Gueft, Olga. "Designing Interiors in an Industrialized World." *Interiors*, January 1957.

Hardy, Charles. "Through the Organizational Looking Glass." *Harvard Business Review*, January-February 1980.

Hughey, Ann. "Social Sciences Help Corning to Design Research Building." *Wall Street Journal*, July 30, 1982.

Josefowitz, Natasha. "Management Men and Women." *Harvard Business Review*, September-October 1980.

Kiechel, Walter, III. "The Self-Absorbed Executive." *Fortune*, December 13, 1982.

_____. "What Your Office Says About You." *Fortune*, May 31, 1982.

Lapp, C.H. "Motivate for Greater Productivity." *Office Management and Equipment*, February 1952.

Leffingwell, W.H. *Making the Office Pay.* 1918.

_____. *Office Management, Principles and Practice.* Chicago: A.W. Shaw Co., 1925.

_____. *Scientific Office Management.* 1917.

Maccoby, Michael. *The Gamesman.* New York: Simon & Schuster, 1976.

"The Magic of Metalizing Business Offices." *The Office Economist*, March 1919.

Mogulescu, Maurice. "Office Design as a Business Proposition." *Interiors*, January 1957.

"Office Furniture: What Do You Need to Know to Be a Smart Specifier for Your Client?" Roundtable discussion reported by *Architectural Record*, mid-February 1982.

"Office Layout and Desk Efficiency." *The Office Economist*, March 1920.

"Office Planning—An Essential to Efficient Management." *The Office Economist*, March 1927.

Peters, Thomas J. and Robert H. Waterman, Jr. *In Search of Excellence.* New York: Harper & Row, 1982.

Pile, John, ed. *Interiors Second Book of Offices.* New York: Whitney Library of Design, 1969.

"Planning the Electronic Office of the Future." *Interior Design*, October 1981.

Rippen, Kenneth. "Lighting Plays a Dynamic Part in Raising Office Efficiency Level." *Office Management and Equipment*, July 1951.

Schumacher, E.F. *Small is Beautiful.* New York: Perennial Library, Harper & Row, 1973.

Whyte, William H., Jr. *The Organization Man.* New York: Anchor Books, Doubleday, 1956.

Index